PRAISE FOR
THE LANGUAGE OF UNBREAKING

"Keana Aguila Labra's *The Language of Unbreaking* is a lyrical odyssey through the labyrinth of identity and heritage, where every verse is a stepping stone on the path to reclaiming self. This collection is necessary and is a dance between the past and the present, a conversation between the known and the unknown."
—**Tshaka Campbell**, Santa Clara County Poet Laureate 2022-2023

"With 'currency in / pasensya, ingat, and holding hands,' Keana Aguila Labra proves that the language of unbreaking is also the language of lament and grief, lineage and kinship, divinity and mortality, place and empire. The beautiful poems in Aguila Labra's debut collection are a generous gift and love letters to homes that span oceans, that transcend geography, and that one finds only in the company of family. Quintessentially Cebuana, quintessentially queer, quintessentially San Jose: This is poetry of care."
—**antmen pimentel mendoza**, author of *MY BOYFRIEND APOCALYPSE*

"Keana Aguila Labra razes language and rebuilds it as her speaker moves in an arc through generations and lineages. With Tagalog and Cebuano phrases, the poet braids memory and talk stories taut with ache and wonder. *The Language of Unbreaking* brilliantly presents an autoethnography of grief and place, inviting us to explore love as landscape, and what ultimately holds a family together."
—**Aileen Cassinetto**, Academy of American Poets Laureate Fellow

"Keana Aguila Labra's poetry is both reverence and rage. Her poems carry us into spaces we may have thought didn't exist, like intimate worlds we only see during low tides. 'How can there be nothing in San Jose when it is everything?' Aguila Labra's new work is a mastery of truth-telling and exploration of what it means to be steeped in diaspora, pamilya, and healing in our daily lives. She works her magic with such lush verse as 'I think often of the coins Lola Baby threw into dirt to bless the house. Her throwing arm the arch of an angel.' We are so incredibly lucky to have her powerful voice."
—**Arlene Biala**, author of *her beckoning hands*, American Book Award winner and Santa Clara County Poet Laureate 2016-2017

"*The Language of Unbreaking*, by Keana Aguila Labra, is a collection of concrete artifacts welded on these delicate and vibrant memories. There is a feeling of their words splitting the atoms of their recollection that dives the reader into these concentrated capsule of emotions. Aguila Labra's love for family, for geographical home, for connection with community is sowed so magnificently through the book. There are moments of loss throughout the book that can destroy a reader's spirit and how it feels like this prescription one has been yearning for. Aguila Labra's body bravely makes its way into poems, at times they are these agononizing autopsies of pain and suffering, to these flesh of joys worth celebrating with each word professed. The Tagalog and the Cebuano language vines and interweaves in many poems, the way nature will gladly reclaim Metropolitan landscapes. *The Language of Unbreaking* is a communion of poetry holding prayers of hope, a dissolving of sin, and a litany of healing."
—**Lorenz Mazon Dumuk**, author of *Held*

"Through the seamless blend of Cebuano and Tagalog, Keana Aguila Labra crafts poems that weave together vibrant, delicate recollections, sometimes anchoring them in physical artifacts that hold profound emotional weight. The words themselves feel like they unravel the very fabric of memory, pulling readers into intense emotional capsules. Aguila Labra's deep love for family, home, and community resonates throughout the book, offering a powerful and heartfelt expression of belonging."
—**Belana Labra**, Sampaguita Press Editor

The Language of Unbreaking

POEMS

Keana Aguila Labra

Sampaguita
Press

The Language of Unbreaking
Published by Sampaguita Press
P.O. Box 731305
San Jose, CA 95127

www.SampaguitaPress.com

Cover and book design: Maria Bolaños & Kelly Ritter
Cover art: Chris Sícat

ISBN 978-1-965439-01-2 (paperback)
ISBN 978-1-965439-04-3 (ebook)

This publication is made possible by funding provided in part by the Montalvo Arts Center, SVCreates, Local Color, and other generous contributions from our readers. We offer our heartfelt thanks for your support.

Masucol means to fight.

—Josefa Cortes Masucol Labra

WHAT IT MEANS TO FOLD

We are paper pleated.
Harsh, humbling, veering,
The curse of mortality.
Where atop are the flowered apologies?
In the spaces, broken.
In our poses, broken.
In our eyes, wilted.
One year did nothing
Two years does nothing
Time is the greatest enemy.
Time, with its tumbling and washing
A wrinkle to mean we are clean, but
A wrinkle here to catch and fall, like
A wrinkle to catch these transitory things.
9 is a 10 in transit
10 is 13 in transit
Questions are transit in reverse
Unknowing is the opposite of grief
The ground weeps at the unknowing
If only we could offer a hand
If only we could reach in
If only we could offer lilied comfort
If only we could be bolstered by white lies
If only we could see the Labra family again,
A family in flux
Unbreaking becoming unraveled
Unbreaking becoming ungrandfathered
Ungrandfathered synonym for unfathered
The cross in my mother's pocket tempts me
The truth is my grandfather's bones beneath me
I'm not yet here, but I will be
The truth a canyon that will only widen
As green as my grandfather's warden
As green imprisons me on the other side.

The Language of Unbreaking

CONTENTS

St Peter and the Wolves

The Unbreaking

I

The Fight of the Baptists

IF YOU WANT TO KNOW WHO I AM,

laugh with butterflies in Lola's garden. Watch the light stream between the clouds off Biscayne. Where Biscayne is pronounced Bis-cay-ne syllables sailed the many miles from San Fernando, Cebu. Follow Biscayne down until you reach brick and dance toward the short stumpen palm men. Remember where the Shakey's is (was) and walk in a single file line along the sidewalk. Never step on cracks. Learn to levitate. Braid your hair until it unfurls into friendship. Into Nancy. Into Jasmeen. Into Jacob. Into Joe. If you find me at Dorsa, please cut the red off the apple's skin. Share these slices with me beneath the shade of gray and blue only San José has during the rainy season. Lola cooked paksiw na isda, so it's time to go. Tuck the seatbelt below your chin and have the window seat cradle you all the way home.

THEY NEVER FUCKING ASK ME "WHERE ARE YOU REALLY FROM" IN EAST SIDE

I'm only twenty miles from home but always
sick of their shit, my arms pulsating rage,
causing time to slow and break down into
its smallest, simplest parts: I am one second
away from "fuck this shit," one impulse from
"fuck this place," one breath away from fucked up.
I return to my prayer, this wetted anger,
and we meet in the autumn.
The origin of us began with a choice,
with Lolo's eyes on a map. If only
they knew the preciousness of this?
How when I see the triptych of McKee,
Alum Rock, then Capitol, I know that I
am home. Yes, our blood is Ilihan,
Mandaue, and San Fernando but
East Side is where he drew his last breath.
So shut your fucking mouth, where I'm really
from. Where I'm from, my neighbors baptize
each other in mariachi. No questions asked,
they lift Lolo from the floor. They wipe the
sweat from his brow. When he is gone, I don't
have to say a word. They already know.

LETTER TO DUTERTE (2018)

IN THE VOICE OF ROMIE ARAÑAS LABRA

PRESIDENT DUTERTE,

I AM WRITING TO YOU ABOUT MY CONCERNS AS YOUR
HUMBLE CITIZEN. AS A DUAL CITIZEN, I HAVE OBSERVED
YOU HAVE OFFERED TWICE THE RESPONSIBILITY AND
NONE OF THE BENEFITS OF BEING A PROUD PINOY. DID
YOU KNOW I NEVER WANTED TO LEAVE MUNTINLUPA?
I DON'T EVEN REMEMBER THE NAME OF THE OFFICER
WHO ADVISED I LEAVE. IF ONLY HE COULD PREDICT THE
HARDSHIP OF DISPLACEMENT. WE IMMIGRATE
OVERSEAS TO IMMIGRATE FROM CITY TO CITY,
APARTMENT TO APARTMENT. I LEFT TO WORK WHEN ALL
MY SON WANTED WAS A FATHER. HOW WOULD I HAVE
KNOWN THAT MY GRANDDAUGHTER WOULD BE BORN
WITH DEEP LONGING? ISN'T THAT THE CONDITION OF
BEING FILIPINO?

DUTERTE, AS A FELLOW VISAYAN, I URGE YOU NOT TO
KILL INNOCENT PEOPLE. WE ARE OWED DUE PROCESS.
WE ARE 500 YEARS OWED. CONSIDER, IN ANOTHER
LIFETIME, WE WOULD BE SEPARATED BY DATU, OUR
WOMEN BELOVED. OUR GENDERS VAST. WE HAVE TO
REMEMBER. YOU WANT POWER? YOU WANT MONEY?
WHAT OF OUR PEOPLE'S SPIRIT? WE ARE NOT LIKE THEM.
WE CANNOT BE LIKE THEM. TAPON IT ALL. NO MORE
GLUTATHIONE. NO MORE THEFT FROM THE PEOPLE.
WE ARE SUPPOSED TO SERVE EACH OTHER. ASA IMONG
KAPWA? YES, WE ARE MEN, BUT ARE WE SO DEVOID
OF SOFTNESS? OF THOUGHTFULNESS? I LOOK AT MY
DAUGHTER-IN-LAW AND SEE HER CURLED FIST. AT MY

ASAWA. PAREJONG NGIPIN SILA SA MGA TIGER. KASI
YEAR OF THE TIGER SILA. BUT ENOUGH OF THAT. THAT'S
MY GRANDDAUGHTER'S FIGHT.

AS VISAYANS, WE HAVE TO HOLD OURSELVES TO A
HIGHER STANDARD SO TAGALOGS IN MANILA WILL
RESPECT US. DO YOU CURL YOUR FIST FOR THIS RESPECT?
SO MANY FILIPINOS HERE CUT THEIR TONGUE TO CURL
TO THE MGA PUTI. I HAVE THREE DEGREES. I'M
EDUCATED YOU SEE. I MOP THE FLOORS AND MY
CHILDREN LOOK AWAY ASHAMED THEIR FATHER IS A
JANITOR. ITONG CLASS ISSUE. RACE ISSUE BA. LIFE IS
EDUCATION, DI BA? NOW I ONLY SPEAK CEBUANO TO
MY WIFE AND CHILDREN. MY CHILDREN ANSWER BACK
IN TAGALOG. MY APO IN ENGLISH. WHAT THEY WILL
REMEMBER OF THEIR PEOPLE? OF ME? BUT ENOUGH OF
THAT. THAT'S MY GRANDDAUGHTER'S FIGHT.

A MAN AS BROWN AS ME SNEERS AT THE YOUTH AND
THEIR PROTEST. IN HIS SNEER HE ASKS IF THEY ARE
ILLEGAL. THIS ACCUSATION MOST MALICIOUS. ANO BA.
DON'T YOU KNOW WE ARE ALL ONE PAPER AWAY FROM
ILLEGAL TO THEM. IT DOES NOT MATTER. SINO BA? WHO
SAID THAT NO MATTER HOW PERFECT NG INGLES KAMI,
WE WILL NEVER BE ONE OF THEM. SALAMAT SA DIYOS
WE WILL NEVER BE WHITE.

DUTERTE, THIS LETTER WAS LONG SENT AND THE FILE
LONG GONE. THE COMPUTER THAT ONCE HOUSED IT
IS GONE. THE HOUSE THAT HOUSED THE COMPUTER IS
GONE. I TOO AM GONE. BUT ENOUGH OF THAT.
THAT'S MY GRANDDAUGHTER'S FIGHT.
THAT'S ON MY GRANDDAUGHTER TO REMEMBER.

MY GRANDDAUGHTER WILL REMEMBER.

YOU KNOW IT'S A CRUSH WHEN YOU START LOOKING INTO ASTROLOGY

Mercury cazimis the sun / and our noses brush. / Once upon a time I was green sweater on green jeans / a tired twenty / rolling earth in search of cover and warmth / and he was / and is / the sun / I knew he was the one when I dug my teeth into his shoulder / I knew he was the one when I laid in his bed and / woke to the realization / I was still enough for sleep / the type of slumber stage enough for peaceful dreaming / I found home in the space between two seasons / I've a newfound
love for summer.

MY COUSIN ALMOST DIED AND NOW I'M SURE SHE'S QUEER

My father taught me how   to jump a car in
the driveway of our home and our neighbors' homes.   Blocked
living means   a protection from the outside. I watched the
neighbor two houses down balloon   from swaddle into cape.
He is the proof of rotation. We cheer at his   arrival, at his
persistence. The trees are our doorman and the   sidewalk
our red carpet. When I turn back to my   father, he is holding
red   and black. Demonstrating. Red to red,   black to
black.   This same cocoon cannot protect us from ourselves.
The way my cousin   almost died is unknown. She a
statue of rope and sweat. A Goliath   felled by nerves
and unseen curses. My ninang calls and   whispers. In
the same swiftness, my cousin is   back on her feet.
She winks at Death as she   chases the sunset. Now, finding
new life, her clothes change name. Red to red, black to black,
she   finds   step   in   this,   bloomed.

I'M MOURNING ON A TUESDAY

I lay in grass and pick blades until I'm 6-years-old again. The clouds were bigger then. My hands were born moving, making elegies of the air. Memory is inextinguishable. It abides by no rules. Its laughs spill through the grates in the steel. Memory starts where folds end, each the concave of writhing flesh. The man at 13 who loses his father again, is the same man who loses his son.

*

If you are born Filipino, you are born to a destiny. If you are born unbreaking, you are chiseled duty. An indent learned you are most loved at the start. Memory makes a ghost of patience. I sing my sins in bark, concrete -- because memory makes friend of regret. Memory the mother of multiple, body refracting a tear moving in reverse. I should have began.

*

I should have ended with the look of an eye -- because memory is a servant of the starts. If you are born writer -- inhale. If you are born daughter -- exhale. This is an appointing inescapable: family writer as historian as coroner. Forget the day.

*

Walk through each house, eyes shut and out. Forget the name of your favorite song but believe your father wrote tong tong tong pakitong-kitong. Know the song in its original Bisaya. An apo loses Lolo again, and again and again -- The message of another holds the self.

*

We hold our wrists out in a way that would make St. Maud smile. If only it were that easy, where match against sinned skin made angel.
When I picture death, he's a man again.
When I picture death, he is Lolo, young.
He is, again.

A PART OF MY HISTORY DIED WITH HIM (LOLO)

AT A PANEL WITH VICTORIA CHANG

Victoria, you summoned him. In
the flat of a Kansas City room,
Lolo wafts in & my chest squeezes.
I've learned that while he is here,
my chest stays tight & I want to cry.
Victoria, I could never hold back
the way my shoulders cleave against
the empty air. I crash into Zoom
rooms trying to find ground.
But here there is nowhere to hide.
Mare holds my knee as if to
know. Victoria, I'm a 6w7 so
you know what I'm looking
for. Everyday I remember that
house is a blessing. When did
we stop marking the wall with
our heights? Just before this, I
held hands with my friends.
Conversation comes to enneagram
and it reminds me I know who I am.
Because I'm a 6w7 I will always fight.
At least, I think so. There is so much I still
don't know. Victoria, my chest is
lightening. At least I know I will always
punch & flail against what I can't control.
When we lost that house is when I
think I lost my footing. When we lost
you, I started to forget the words.
Victoria, I use your name but who I
really mean is Lolo. Lolo,
please stay. Please stay.

THE CHILD OF BUTCHERS

Lola at Lolo, the magkakarne. Nay takes tongs to the head. The singit. Above it all, my Nay is my Nay when she pushes and tells me to look away. The crabs thrash and claw, seconds between life and death. On most days, I don't get this Nay when I remember that my Nay is forty-nine wrapped around fifteen, the way that abandonment becomes a shell hardened. A bomb shelter. I reach my hand in asking her to take me in. But all she knows is to close the door.

"WE USE LANGUAGE TO SIGNIFY WHO OUR HOME IS."

—KARLA SANTIAGO-REYES

The house where Cathay meets Loyola
is born a god. Is born a choice.
Fingers that chose place, paint
and person. Where red becomes
beige below brown, and the god
realizes they're born of mortals.
Minor deities and their guards,
feline eyes of warning. Kneel
each morning a humble offering
of Krispy Kreme. Sidewalks of
eternity, sneakers in appreciation and
knowing. This universe, this design
of atomic pooling was the most
beautiful. Where god's scooter is met
with waves and smiles. Around the corner
is Pops. Back up are the Titans, the Royals,
a smack and chew that can only be described
as intimidating. How can there be nothing
in San Jose when it is everything?

Ito Na, Para Kay Lola, Amping

Gumagising si Lola mga 9 o 10 sa umaga these days / Akyat ni Lola sa
kwarto ko kasi umaga sa akin is late for her / we are kusog kaayo /
always reaching for the sun / until her knee falls victim to gout / ito
na, / this / is how we once upon a time / in East Side San José /
perfect and Taglish / or more accurately Cebtaglish or Bistaglish or
Taguanolish or Tagsaylish / Because in this house, / our house / we
split grammar like bread / haloed these languages, wheat and brown /
Tagalog Cebuano and English / though blended / is whole / Our lips
/ wolves, / which is to say there is a wholeness in breaking. / which is
to say we break but do not separate / I believe she is the answer / she
/ Lola, Grandma, / our center / is grain / dirt / and sky and everyone
/ I take her with me / shared in the eyes of dodong who calls me inday
/ inday as princess / as lady / as shapeshifter / as in inday does not
mean maid / and inday ages into she who the youth call manang / she
who is bandaid on green helmets / brown boots and fang to misplaced
hate / which is to say / she / is good intention / she / is wolf mother,
wolf anchor, / indomitable will as unrelenting fist because / she
refuses to walk in the winter. / So, we exercise / around the kitchen
and I learn to steel my skin every time / she tapons another one of my
dishes. / On these days, I miss Lolo the most. / Which is to say / we
/ miss Lolo the most / the master of chicharon's talsik / conductor
of wolvish orchestra / and symphony of smacking / in delight despite
skill or taste / but in the celebration of food / which is to say I was
raised in gratitude / My ears long for the simplest exchange / quick and
gahi where direct translation / is not necessary / and these ears feel
to understand / where Cathay and Loyola meet and become Ilihan /
Mandaue / and San Fernando, Cebu / each word marbling as it touches
air becoming sound / my tongue yearning to wrap around its staccato /
this kundiman of want / because what is weekend without neighbor /
and mariachi / and the pitterpatter jazz of the rain / and how it mimics

the speed of Lola's voice / how our chins bow when we say / uulan / I catch it and with its permission let it sit on my teeth / and travel to my bones / because I thank god for Google Maps and its image history / so I can go back to February 2020 / and see the house as it was when it was ours / this / is what we lose in passing / this / is what I keep on this earth that was his. / And I can't properly describe in this language or the next / the loss of a keeper who didn't pass down the key / I am born from their wheat but / how do I break into bread? / I gut my insides in the hopes of finding seeds / but my pare waves his hand / a beckon / and we sit in this / bahay de pan / in this pan de buhay / because I am hija de pan/ and he / reminds me to be patient for what I know is wit and love, / for what I feel is home. / and in my palms are ambots as offerings, / I nod no and laugh bitaws. / I promise tsismis to all my Ates / Kuya / manong ug mga kaibigan / because tanan and tayo means we / Letter to letter lined with our being, / each word the sampaguita'd stitching of us. / fairy tale becomes prayer / a prayer of forgiveness / a prayer of peace / in the name of her / apo / and the holy spirits / Lola ug Nana / Lola at Nini / my grandma and me.

KUNDIMAN FOR MARTY DELGADO

I'm always longing for home, so much so my friends let me sing of San José until my voice is hoarse. The same way they let me sing of the Josefa and Josef before me. They know my Lola Josefa as Josie. This is how we denote family, by the way we know names. They love her, too. They think of her hands atop her belly and movies of vengeance and feel her strength. So, Marty, just this once I'll sing for you. Kasi meaning yung yan, this Kundiman. Leave it to our people to blend beauty with freedom. Let me tell you a story. The story begins in the sky. I saw our beloved Pacific and thought of you. How we talked about keeping cultures and fathers. My father was once a boy, was once Cebuano. I catch him sometimes, eyes closed in the kitchen, and I swear I can tell he's thinking of the archipelago. I miss this father I never knew. These are the things we decide to keep to ourselves. But promise me you'll tell me about how your father's fathers fingers feel. How do they tell the story of grass? Promise me you'll tell me his name. Lola's lola is now unnamed. I think that's the greatest tragedy. To go unknown, to go unloved. More importantly, there are more lessons to learn. I have to tell you a secret. We're cousins after all. My grandfather and your grandfather the same. As I looked down upon the Pacific, the waves were made in the shape of your name.

Paksiw na Isda ni Lola

Lola births herself on the plate. White and green
vine worship the steaming and flayed.

She picks tinik, placing plastic and film atop tissue.
Every bone removed atonement. A promise.

Lola crouches and I believe when she stands,
her hair brushes the ceiling and therefore God.

I think, one day, I too will tiptoe touch this ceiling
and therefore God. I was born into this fight.

I stare at myself in the mirror and push rice
and fish onto spoon. I eat to be in conversation.

I eat in remembrance of names.

I eat to come home.

II

Spidered Deference

Create yourself

with every inhale.

—Maria Bolaños

I COME FROM CRUELTY

A curse begins with longing

solution molded from flesh,

so what happens when sticky skin becomes mouthed

and unwanting?

A curse born with purpose

a curse realized as destiny defied –

scarred sagittarius, a blazing moon

its heat enough to distract from its heavy

hung from a wide handed sky,

When I said death is a man like Lolo,
I meant it as counter,

I meant it as welcome.

Please, O, God,

please spare this flesh from being lesson,

for flesh is as earth is the birthplace of life.

I committed the sin of emerging from

                    the grand canyon of her,

where I learn wind whipped that there is

                    no room for me anywhere.

Please, O, God,

                    may I instead be born from softer gardens,

Nay – may I instead trade my legs to stay

                    but a moment's glimmer in that wide handed sky.

PERSON OF PRAYER

I prayed to grow, to be woman'ed. I thought of those boys' hands
and thought not of me. It was never about me. I don't need prayer to
shrink everything else, but still. I dab extra holy water and pray harder
to be smaller, a recurring plan then and now. Make me skinny, make me
silent, make me perfect. Let this one act change me. It's time to eat this
god who is not my god, which is another rule I break. I am the end of
my family line, quivering with excitement. I refuse the cross. The priest
speaks, the body of Christ, and lays him on my tongue. I take him in,
eyes closed.

Changed by prayer,
my god, of God, a man.
It's always a man.

Virgo Szn Starts in a (Virgo) Mercury Retrograde

A body lays against the fold
>A body still with a mind in outpour

A life of contradictions
>Absent / Present mother

Ring around the posies
>Stuck in again, again, again

A Venus Retrograde
>Nine years walks a tight rope

A Saturn Return
>A perilous claw to self

THE BUTCHERS

Lola at Lolo, the magkakarne. Pupunta dito, galing sa Tondo. Isn't this important too, I thought, as I held my phone to this Lolo's lips. What other ways to separate the two? My Lolo died and this is an action of hindsight. I try to tell this Lolo of what part of me is buried with him, but I'm pulled away the moment this Lolo says I still have one. The way my mother begs now is the same way she begged to stop rolling embutidos. There are no embutidos in the house now, no Simbang Gabi. But I understand why moms need god in their house.

LIFETIMES ARE MADE IN A SPRING

Time the meadow where the newborn calf lays
a figure of legend and tragedy.
I am a youth divided,
my hands in the future
head in the past. So
this is the monster's Shape.

On rare occasions, we occupy
the same space at the same time,
a kitchen dance of child and adult
mirroring the child in adult.
I am constantly looking.
I am an elder misguided.
I look at my hands aghast at the lines.
I have undone, I am undone.

Here, where the lions beat their paws against clouds
a cry of defiance across space and time.
The wind visits a while.
Never before has my feet moved so much in vain.

A LIST OF IMPORTANT MEMORIES

I love choosing more than one toy / at the $0.99 store in Tracy / I gravitate toward cute stuffed toys / or pens / or diaries / I love / having leftovers from a large meal / fridge bursting at the seam / in what our families / promise is love / I watch the sunset / and think of ghosts / who wouldn't be / happy / with the storm brewing inside / my palms / a storm / I tend / daily / I love the wind / as it caresses / each windmill / and kisses Lola's flowers / and the hush of papers / from an open book / I love the still / between 12am and 1am / right when my virtual Cebuano class ends / because they're based in Melbourne / and there's a time difference / before I even set down my headphones / I know / Lolo is sleeping. / I step outside to grab my books / and journal / and Lolo is snoring. / I tiptoe toward the main bedroom / stepping over the creaky floorboard, / but never before whispering / goodnight.

BAPTISTS' GOLD

I used to live in Tracy. My siblings and I would say the LR in Lawrence Ranch actually meant Labra Residence. Exit 11th St and turn right at the light. Turn left and go straight until you reach the corner house.

*

I was in a combination 5th and 6th grade class at George Kelly with Ms. Brown and another teacher. I don't remember her name anymore, but her daughter's name was Quinn. I would listen to the Pussycat Dolls CD in the bathroom and wish my name was Quinn, too. I would rep red track so hard.

*

Auntie Ricci would pick me up from school, and I would confess to her my crushes in my rosy roundness asking her why I'm ugly. She instead would reach for my hand and tell me I am so beautiful.

*

In the Tracy house, my room was pink and I had a princess tower. My sister and I alternated between sleeping in her blue room, back to back, and together in lamplight in my room. We would lock our brother out of my closet, claiming we were in Dragon Land. I closed my eyes and imagined the coats as rainbow scales.

*

We practiced our ears and tongues at the local Boyong. Lola Baby started a Tagalog diary with me and she translated every single thing for me. Dami. Pawis. Aso. Lola. I was blessed with abundance.

*

We lost Stitch in this house. We met Nina in this house. All of my grandparents played tongits in this house. I keep this house in my heart. I visit all its rooms freely.

*

I think often of the coins Lola Baby threw into dirt to bless the house. Her throwing arm the arch of an angel. We drove to the lot in the middle of the night and threw coins onto the ground. The coins still there. The coins as witness. The coins as legacy. The coins proof of us.

ENOUGH

Before I realize I do not,   cannot become a doctor,
I am one: stitching together letters as an ode to the moon,
during a time when all poets who were meant to be poets
fall in love with her   quiet. Before I realize that choosing
~~for~~ myself meant choosing discord, the fabric of confessions
spilled   in-between   chores from red to blue line and
droplets from faucet to towel to plate to an innocent, yet
foreboding notebook. because I, too, promised my mother,
and I will learn   not   to stumble over my own tongue.
If I cannot find the love I want, I will give it to myself.
Before I realize that youth is not the end all, be all, when I
realize there is in fact Time and plenty of it for all that I am
destined to become,

Then-
and only then.

NEUR()DIVERGENT DIARY

()
I hate this mind
I hate this body

()
I cry to my best friend outside of the garage
because I surpass my allowance of fuck-ups

()
And beyond that, I cry to my laptop alone
because again I surpass my allowance of fuck-ups

()
Curse this brain
curse this lack of

()
I count these fuck-ups on one hand
Three is the magic number

()
Three, like my mother used to say
to the count of three

()
Trouble has a way of finding me
A soulmate is a mirror

()
The person I love the most tells me
I get worse every year

()
Another reason to fear age
Another reason to look away

◊
My palms
How much hate can I hold?

◊
How many days
until my fuck-ups are forgiven?

◊
How many days
until I'm wiped clean

◊
until I'm whole
until I'm human?

"IN MY GRIEF, I'VE CHANGED & THAT'S OKAY"

Everyday, I choose to perfect the art of self-soothing. 15minute blue dot definition of virgo tells me to listen. Slow down. On my best days, I close my eyes and pretend these stick straight letters are my mom: "I'm so proud of you." On my worst days, I know it's my mom: "I'll always be here for you." & everyday I dream up Westerns undercover smiling to myself knowing even deities themselves pray to gods. So when I beg him for finality, I'm grateful to awake to my hands. Not all that is said is true. Something is changed with truth, yes, but truth is the kind-eyed gentleman that offers to stow away your baggage without expectation. I am tethered to the blinking millipede of hope standing between myself and the man whose chin upturned transforms stoicism to a flood. I sit at the window seat having known blessing first-hand. I try to share this blessing with others. With you. They say resentment is holding a knife to your throat & my arms are tired. I lay my palms at my lap. I exchange this time for mine & take in the sunrise with a smile.

PORTRAIT OF THE LUNA MOTH & ITS MISSING MOUTH

The luna moth begins as a hungry caterpillar. New to life, new to its place in the Americas, it feasts on the abundance of walnut, hickory, sweet gum, and paper birch trees. The ritual of the cocoon begins after this sacred month. It dives, tucks, and sleeps. Then it is born again. While originally insatiable, it now finds itself without: without mouth, without digestive system. Its life now ticking; it only lives for a week after its slumber in the cocoon. For the rest of its life, it never eats.

I.

I was born hungry. I was born wanting. Two weeks old, my body so insatiable it burst across the belly, flesh wondering where to go, flesh wondering where it would be held.

II.

My mother's voice the walnut, my Lola's laugh the hickory, my father's arms the gum, and my siblings each paper birch trees. Lolo, our cocoon, holding his apo as much as he could fit in his arms.

III.

I am no moth. Born hungry, still hungry. I am only mouth. My belly still warps under pressure, its crease the proof of a life wanting to live.

III

The Chord of Eagles

A daughter is a burning candle.

—Maria Bolaños

I WOULD RATHER FIGHT A HURRICANE

Once I broke all my uncle's cigarettes and flushed them down the toilet,
its swirls an enrapture that taught me how to separate my mind from my body. Where I,
still mercury, became gemini'd in a way that would horrify Flannery O'Connor,
but my memory is awful, so who knows who wrote the story of which I'm thinking?
All I know is that this was the first time I saw the consequences of what it means to be
human, whorling flesh of blood pump and sinew. And my uncle, though full of love,
became filled with this and in his hands became doubled the way that sons
Learn their rage from their father. But I've never felt regret for that
day, instead rather citing it as one of my shining moments of bravery --
picture a girl of twelve with round cheeks and round belly storming
her uncle's room to kill that which is killing him because I've yet to
Learn the word HIV so what else could the sakit Nay speaks of be
other than these sticks that we learned about from Darren the lion?
What I don't tell people is the story after the story. How, he cried
and hugged me and kissed my forehead. How, he still had
another pack of cigarettes in his backpack anyways. How,
he climbed the stairs to the front door with my back to the
soft click until I found myself peeking through the window.
I watched his artistry. My uncle, who like me, is mercury'd,
swayed like the wheat we are. My uncle, who taught me
how to braid my hair, his cheeks meeting his eyes when
he said it was okay to like boys as long as I remember
God. How, now I wondered where god was for him?
How, now I know that he was thirty-two holding a
painful truth. A lonely truth. How, now I wish I
had gone to him. But the truth is, I watched.
Watched the dance of his shoulders, up
and down, knowing that the back
heaving is another way a son
longs for his father.

BABY ___

- Any flesh that spills from your hand is too much.
- Googling, "how to be seen as me beneath the folds?"
- You gain 10 pounds.
- Flesh sitting is flesh rotten.
- Will you find god in these Google searches?
- The ground where I bury my flesh is loud with the shape of me,
- You gain 10 pounds; you're overweight.
- Waiting to be called hottie, baddie, from eyes who don't see you as such
- The void's retort: do you see you as such?
- The truth is I was prettiest back then, so
- I time travel to 10 more pounds and baby.
- I memorize the prayer of you:
- "O Hallowed Ground, It is But Another Thing I Don't Like About You."
- Wanting to be held.
- Contemplating why?
- I am jello flesh wanting to be called pretty.
- What is pathetic but unwanted flesh, waiting
- I emerge from the language of mourning.
- Googling, "what does it mean if my body makes me want to die?"
- Goal post comparison of past and present,
- Googling, "have you ever felt naked rejection?"
- Back in the present, I am jealous.
- Replaying, "so you want me to lie?"
- Stomach too big, stomach too ugly
- Body too big to fuck.
- Where's Jesus when you need him most?
- Another prayer of you:
- "O Flesh of Body, You Were the One Who Changed On Me."
- Contemplating the difference between mother and incubator,
- How much of me remains in this future imagined?
- Googling, "how do I know if I'm understood?"
- What does it mean to want? Waiting,
- Which is to say, what I don't want to be:
- Flesh that envelopes flesh.

A MAN WITH A HAT GETS ON AT THE STOP,

and Lolo visits us on this bus.
He laughs loud and talks loud
with the driver. He tells his stories slowly, to build

anticipation. Then he tells his stories again,
the way we know
them, the way we've heard before.

But he is silent when no one wants to talk
anymore, anticipating
grief. I am holding

my phone, but I am listening
holding
what he says, then what he does not say.

At Rockaway,
there is a pull on a heartstring
and the bus doors open

the same way
I feel
a heart might break.

I'm DONE BETRAYING MYSELF

I feel this vow in my bones.

I take my beauty and hold it close to my chest.

I, this hottie. I, this baddie.

I, this beautiful person in layered flesh.

I give myself new name.

This flesh that holds me, protects. I cry, not at his words anymore, but at the sight of me. Each tear a promise deepening. How could I not see it before? I understand now what my kasamas mean when they say we each are a little perfection. I see a post on Instagram that begs women to see the god within themselves. I thank them for reaching me across digital space. I take the unwanted seeds and remove them from the dirt of me. I learn alchemy in the bathroom on the second floor. This is history. On my twenty-ninth year, I refuse the comparisons. I make my own ideal. I begin the undoing. I mourn. Not for me. For him. And what he is beginning to lose. Each seed goes up in flame. He tells me I am not as beautiful as I was before. I look directly into my eyes and mouth a curse. Some gods are born again. I breathe in my new skin.

LOVE AS A BUTTER SANDWICH

I
Today I cleaned piss off the floor,
yellow unspooling faster than my tissue
closing my eyes and reaching for another on instinct.
Tomorrow I return, at least to an expected rhythm:
the leaves will be green, the oranges orange
and my lolo as sour as my lola's lemons.
That was the thing: there was gratitude
thank yous said generously, but it was
the action preceding:
thank you, after a change of clothes
thank you, after keeping coil in cup
thank you, after placing each pill
accordingly based on
time, blood pressure, and heart rate.
Doing as I'm thinking of my lover's lips,
his texts consistent since September of 2014,
amazing what power these tender
anchors hold.

II
Last night, I gave
my lolo a second pill of Benadryl
so I could sleep.

My hands moved before anything else
within me could say no. The night wind
shaking the walls, the computer in my
aunt's old room humming as if to say
you're not alone.

And here, inside San José, the lights
are so beautiful. The holiday
twinkling, as if taking turns,
as if we were woven together

an extended family.

III
Then, there is the worn granddaughter
hauling her laptop to the table.
The grandmother always
Moving,

always
Looking.

If there aren't leaves to be swept,
then there are flowers to water,

clothes to be washed,
insulin to be administered,

and the grandmother's back
curls in response, as if to

beg for rest.

But, where there is Selfish
there are the Selfless

and she returns
to the kitchen
and emerges with
a sandwich.

IV
Love---

beyond family, obligation
utang na loob and
duty,

I take you in with each bite.

THE BODY IS OUR BODY UNTIL IT IS NOT OUR BODY

We are one with blood.   We are born with this audience, which is to say we follow the moon. We drink   from the fountain of our mothers and its salt   a reminder of how these things are passed down. These things that coagulate   and fester. Our mothers   regurgitate to ensure we are fed, but we are void. Which is to say, we are born lacking.   We know what was taken from us.   Which is to say, we are brought into this world with the intent of   leaving us a little empty. The mother who is my mother is also the girl   abandoned. She is the girl scrutinized, love withheld.   Left   to her own devices, left to newness. New family. New land. New language.   There is no mercy for us.   We were told that language comes from the body, but how   many times were our bodies imagined by another mind? We are sacrificed as Prometheus.   We are picked clean. They take our hands, chest,   and miles of skin to tear and take apart. They stitch and it becomes their hands.   Their chest.   Their new miles of skin. We are   ground until made salve, until we are nowhere to be found. Because the mother who is my mother is also the mother who picks her teeth with my   bones. Who declares me too much to carry.   But blood is made into water. Our mothers'   betrayal is what we wash from our hands. We are clean. We were always clean.   See, I was sacrificed as Prometheus but I forged myself Heracles. A prayer returns the water to the sea. We create and protect.   We make our mercy.   We fold forgiveness into our pockets. The fountain   sinks and our daughters emerge in search of the sun. Our daughters emerge as one, their hands out for blood. We crane our necks to their rays.   We   smile, blinded   by   their   light.

ALL SOULS' DAY

Midway between eclipses,
lolo comes home. Even here,
he is positioned towards the sun.
He basks in it. I wait, at ease, by
the tree. It was like this, even then,
when he and I would sit - a recliner
and couch facing the TV as the sun
set on our Cathay Drive home. This,
a time, when the light spilled over
everything ours: floor, walls, picture
frame. This is the day we choose
for our reunion. I am set in motion.
I flip through the pages in my book
shaking my head at Jack, sisters, and
snow. Lolo is watching me, content
at our being. We are held by presence.
As the sun passes over moon, he holds
my gaze. It's time. I know this type of
rain by the way it pulps the pages.
When will I see you again? He is
unblinking. He does not answer.
Neither do I. We know there
are no saints. At least, this
time, there is no lowering into
ground. I promise there is only
ascendance. The eclipse is over
and the sun makes one last
reach. At the end of this day,
Lolo nods at me, at my book.
"Is it any good?" which is to
say, arcs must meet their end
because the morning my brother
was born, the wood shone cold a
mirror. It opened to Lolo's back,
straight and eager, ever waiting
for us to come home.

DIDN'T I SAY WE ALL DESERVE LOVE?

First, we take 1 bowl, ceramic and Mulan'd. Which is to say, she and
I and it were always meant to carry. Take a handful of the moon
and the family's pride and dice finely into bowl. A dash of ginger to
keep sickness away. A dash of garlic for taste. As my mother sleeps,
I steal a tear and mix. I take my father, as a child, and peel away
at the abandonment. I use its petals as garnish. I move this bowl
mountainside on the night of a full moon. I pick 3 chrysanthemums
into water. I let it wash all over me. I julienne a memory of best friends
and am transformed, thirteen.

Thirteen, when I took knife to board and counted into oblivion, its
monotony protecting me from the talsik and the things more painful
that seep from my skin and the skin before me and the skin before
them. Thirteen and thinking if I stand far enough away from the heat I
would be safe. But a leaf born from the tree is not defined by the tree. I
raise my arms at the night sky, holied and starred, arms a wicked sword.
This leaf and I dance. This leaf with each line distinct. It dislodges
from the tree atop the wind but it is always homed. Chin upward, I
shed this skin of skins. Now what do we have? May we always peer
deeply. In our bowl is everything, the recipe complete. It was always
here. My mother's tear is more than wet. And I am more than daughter.

WE'RE AT THE MET AND I'M THINKING ABOUT DEATH

I always start with mistakes.
I live in the before and future,
body pulled so far there is no
now. There is a man, checkered
cap, using charcoal and china
marker documenting a time long
gone, and I am here with my fingers
and notes app holding hands
with Lolo. There is a song of
New York, a song of him and auntie,
who was a girl before an aunt,
a daughter before an aunt,
and I see them hand-in-hand.
In this way, we're here together
separated by 25 years. But
together again, nonetheless.

SIMBANG GABI PARA SA MGA PUTI

Ano daw?
Help me to understand
what we get to keep
when these cats mew for
those who will not return.

Midnight mass?
Please, god.
I was born from a question,
Descended from defiance,
my knuckles bear the same bruises,
lolo and I tilt the same crown.

Bakit meron silang
Simbang Gabi sa Easter? Ano ba yan?
Kasi their fears can only be found
in the imaginary, whereas our fears
are realized in white. In sacrament. In
grass. In dirt. In return. Where only here can
mare's uncles can be lolo's neighbors.

Mercy. Tissues in bloom. Currency in
pasensya, ingat, and holding hands.

Ang Tatay ng Nanay ko, hinawak niya
ang kamay ko. Ang sabi niya,
you still have one. Sinabi ko,
I will always have two.

Please have mercy on us.

LINEAGE

On my father's paternal side, there is a legend of our surname's origin. 'Labra', stemming from the Spanish 'Labrador', a single ancestor, a thief and a rebel, successfully fled Spain. There are no details spared: we don't know his first name nor his city of origin. We only know his intent: he needed to get away. He shortened his name to avoid capture. Lolo doesn't know why our ancestor chose the Philippines, or if it were a choice at all. Perhaps the archipelago, this cluster of islands, were simply happenstance.

I am filled with vigor and pride for this lone man; how thrilling it is to be related to a rebel, to have been born from his supposed courage... until Lolo describes how this same ancestor forced himself upon one of the Filipinos and she bears him twelve sons and one daughter.

This ancestor could not have known (or perhaps he did, making it worse) the splintered identity, or lack thereof, of the Indigenous Filipino people. They did not even refer to themselves as 'Filipino' until the Spanish occupation, as the Spanish claimed our land as theirs, dubbing us, 'La Isla Filipinas.'

But, Lolo tells me this story, so I know to be kind to anyone whose surname shares ours. 'Labra', also meaning unbreakable in its new country. He tells me this because he laments having six granddaughters from his sons. He voices his languish so blatantly in front of my sister and I.

I often wonder about the thirteenth daughter, where my distant cousins are and how they're faring. I also wonder about the Filipina, and how I don't know her name. I don't know how I may honor her.

IV

St Peter and the Wolves

I'll run as if I'm afraid

but know you've made me fearless.

—Eric Asuncion

TERABITHIA

Here we stay at the cusp of adolescence,
where our cries are only in joy
and our mothers are sisters
and holidays routine and peaceful.

Harmony stays beneath quilted blankets
and we fall asleep on the floor to scary movies
where we are picture perfect
and fear is behind a plastic screen.

The space between seasons grow longer,
and we stand in the green every year shorter. But here,

our laughter is frozen in time,
a gift to the neighbors, for it is a gift
we can no longer claim for ourselves.

KUYATE EMAILED THE POEM THEY WROTE FOR THEIR MA, AND I WAS HELD

Mornings were for mischief. Saturdays began with a stealth that only Masucols had. Lola Cadia, the matriarch of us, summoned the sun with her hands. I was a girl born into a family of plenty. I had Lolas the number of one hand, more than any other girl that I knew in my kindergarten class of twenty students. But girls aren't immune to favoritism, and Lola Cadia was my favorite.

Lola Cadia and I were the gods of kulit. It was in our every action. It was in the way we smiled at each other; Masucol girls knowing without having to say. But I was a Masucol girl severed. A line of proud, square-shouldered women with Bisaya as tongue and blade bore me but a hilt. So these mornings began in quiet: I with no Bisaya and Lola Cadia with no English. We were all body: swift through the kitchen, hands in candy jars, and the ceremony of unwrapping. Plastic confetting to the floor as delight melted atop our tongues. We Bisaya are never without our rituals.

The night Lola passed, she visited me in a dream. It is family legend that she did so to say good-bye to her apo before she began her forty day journey. When I woke and told my family my dream, my mother's hand flew to her mouth faster than any gunslinger in Lola's westerns. There was no need to put one finger down, but I did. Separated by twenty-four years, Lola Cadia visits me again.

This time, in adulthood, she visits and stays a while. Kuyate's mother passes, and they email me a poem. Their mother and Lola Cadia moving and laughing in the same way described that I try to do the math thinking I've proof of reincarnation. On my phone, in my hands, rests the incantation for one last visit. Eyes and hands before me again the way we Masucol girls arrive, arms outstretched. The Masucol girls reminding me of our lineage, how Masucol means to fight. Lola Cadia, ghostly and forever, nods and I stick out my tongue. Upon it, she places a tootsie roll. It melts in my mouth the same as it did all those years ago, a ritual that continues for the things we never said.

An Ode to Leos Who Love Virgos

No one offers forgiveness the way
flame holds your hands.
Fire has a way of soothing calloused rock,
despite the rock's grooved and weeping cruelty.
This fire is not afraid to press forehead to forehead
stoking a warmth enough to bring tears
to stoicity. Fire carries fire when rock
cannot. Its lick remind rock that life
is a blessing in itself. Lick as campfire,
As punch, as wildfire. This is the kiss of the sun,
while the rock looks on, in awe. This stellium
tempered by oxen, air, and wheat.
In time, fire will marry rock, and the sky will
crackle under their transformation, their
renewal. There is nothing more breathtaking
than the purity of good intention, of his goodness.
Of rain arranging itself upon gentle mane while he
laughs at the water, making him all the more beautiful.

HOW WILL YOU / HAVE YOU PREPARE(D) FOR HIS DEATH?

He holds my hand. / We watch a special on Netflix / examining conflict in relationships. / His hold does not waver. / I am a blanket of worries, / tapestry worn and frayed, / untying that which does not serve me. / He carries these strands in the light. / His hold does / not waver. / In this special, this couple writes a number / a percentage of how much / they want to be together. / I split / at their 70% / and 80% / a deer that raises their ears at the wind / a danger that is not present / but knowing the breath is a force born from a body that / could / become / danger. / Still / his hold / does not waver. / I leave and park at Safeway / errands redirecting static. / The theory of the multiverse / means a freedom of choice / where these paths become the maze / of all "what could have beens" / but in this time / in this life / I unfold a piece of paper / strategically placed in my purse / sharpie tang in my nose / and I cry at its curves / I cry unraveled / at its / his / 100%.

HEL(L)ION AS PERFECT FAMILY

Where nakedness is
another form of laughter,
where touch is shared not taken.
Charging ions as response.
As synonym to dilated pupils.
Routine is appealing on paper,
but structure is
built from skin on skin.
In conversation. How does
lightning travel across teeth?
Throated storms
the mother of promise.
I mistook he as Helios
when he is he as hellion.
What if he is both?
What if fusion meant
future in simplicity?
In the kissing of palms.
In laying down our arms.

LOLA SAYS WALA KO KABALO BUT WHAT SHE REALLY MEANS IS SHE DOESN'T REMEMBER

Memory makes person : person makes place : that makes home : that makes memory : if memory makes person then what is person : without : place? : if place is trigger for : memory : what happens to : the basis : of person? : what if wall is cradle : as mother is to warmth? : what if heater is mimic : of lolo's snore? : what if hallway : is reminder fears are overcome : what if gravel is relief Dad is home? : what if western is : translated Bisayan curses? : what if volume turned up : sound touching every room : is lullaby? : where will I keep : what new where : will fit my : hands? : what space : will be enough : what space : to be still : what space : to hold : what space : to remember : we were : here?

Deepest Condolences to the Labra Family

In which we are pearls. In which we bear a cross. Inri. In remembrance. In spilling. In heaving. Each of us nailed at the spine. In which we all wear white. In which we all might share the same last name or wherein last name is middle name. Regardless. Only we wear white. Only we as in this branch, gnarled purple wood and yellow. In which my brother is broken into powder blue pieces. In which I have to tell my baby cousin to say his good-byes. Where when I hold him, I am holding myself.

In which I promise to always tell them stories of him.
In which now Lolo lives in kingly wings. White wings.

The sun cries its light down to us.

It tells me we are pearls.

It tells me this cross is worth its weight.

It tells me in remembrance.

It tells me he is everywhere alive.

ONLY AN (AGUILA) LABRA WOULD FIGHT GOD, WHICH IS TO SAY ONLY I WOULD FIGHT GOD

Because / where were you / when Lolo fell / and I wanted to scream against / his weight because I could not carry him / but I needed to / because no one / else was there / and I did it / because I needed to. / why were my sister and I there / cleaning out home after childhood home / a test of tolerance and faith / so now our skeletons sparkle in the sun / so much of my existence / is because / someone needed me to / and I can't see myself living outside of / what others need me to / because what about when / I need you too? / god / I needed you / when I crossed / the street / eyes down to Mr. Max's 3rd grade class / at Dorsa / and he laughed and said / honey, you could've been / hit by a car / begging is like constantly being / hit by a car / each impact morphs / please god / into fuck you god / fuck / you / god / where were you / why did you / take my lolo / why / god / please / God / our sorrow is / too much.

I KEEP SAYING THE SAME THING BUT IT'S OKAY

Sometimes my tongue cuts me from the inside.
Sometimes my partner says.
Sometimes there's no reason to wear skin as shield.
Sometimes I'm silent.
Sometimes my thoughts run together, inconsolable.

Sometimes we start on a preschool ceramics class.
Sometimes I'm in a box of mirrors.
Sometimes the children stomp and scream.
Sometimes unfiltered. I am mirror turned inside out.
Sometimes their tears are free, wild.

Sometimes I am clay. I don't know how to tell a story.
Sometimes I am clay before the kiln. Failing before I've even begun.

I ONLY EVER PRAY ON THE PLANE

Please god, I don't want to die.

I think of my dad's love for Clark

Kent and Superman and chuckle at

our fear of turbulence, this irony white

knuckled fear brewing bravery.

But the cabin shakes, and I'm so

scared. My love is a thousand

miles away. My home is a

thousand miles away. Please

god, I don't want to die. In my dad's

favorite episode of Justice League

Unlimited – which is also mine –

Superman fights Darkseid.

In this episode, Superman tells

Darkseid everyday he lives in a

cardboard box. This, a misnomer

a mis-remembrance. A world of

cardboard becoming a box. These are

the kind of things that stay with me.

I think it's the same for Dad.

A lot of things make me cry but

especially him. There's too much

to say. Mana kay tatay ko kasi

mahirap to explain so we don't

explain it. Action takes place of words.

What does it mean to heal?

I guess that's why I became a poet.

Alum ko na what it means to do

the best you can. "It's okay, Nini" is

sometimes the I love you. "I know, Dad"

is sometimes the I love you too.

I'm okay reaching toward this middle.

I have a confession.

I still call him Daddy the same way

he called Lolo Daddy until he passed.

Lolo stays in Daddy's

hands. Did Lolo think of him

before he left this world?

god, this cardboard box

is so precarious. So precious.

Superman, did you know I'm

Kal L too? Hyphenated identity

and all. At least I know the sound

of Cebuano. I can't imagine the

grief of missing a language you've

never heard. Anyways. Thank you for

letting a Filipino liken themself Superman.

See, god, I can't die yet.

I have a legacy to uphold.

One day, my son will too be Clark.

I close my eyes in this middle seat

as we toss and turn, feeling the strength

in my palms. My breathing

slows. I begin to believe we'll

be okay. I think of Superman.

Is this how he felt the

first time he flew in his cape,

in the letter and language of his

people? Was he also thinking

of his father?

Maybe just maybe.

BUTCHERED CHILD

Baby at Eddie the magkakarne.

It's muscle memory now.

Nay takes tong to head.

The crab flinches at her touch.

Crab, vision of cancer, crab in my placement of mars.

I flinch before her hand even touches my face.

V

The Unbreaking

It's not about what

we deserve.

—Eric Asuncion

DEAR PACIFIC,

Pacific, thank you. Thank you for your bounty. Your arms that touch the shores of homes and connect us. Thank you for my mother. My father. Lola and Lolo.

—

I remember the way you held my body buoyant as I peered at the life below me. I know where I come from, and we come from you. May we seek the freedom you embody. May we find peace in all that you bring. May I always find home in you.

—

Ocean, salamat. Gikan kanimo, kami natawo. Usa ko ka bata sa kadagatan sa Turtle Island. Bata ko sa kadagatan nga nangandoy sa Sugbo.

—

Love,

Aguila, Labra, Masucol, Arañas, Bautista, Lopez, Galang, Romano, and all that we were named in the before

I WANT TO DIE AND I'M THINKING OF WASHBOARD ABS

Pigfaced butcher god takes pity on me, so I die quickly. The rest steel tongues on cutting blocks who bow sacrifice to the god of molting. Somewhere beneath lard laden is beauty. Hands deep, eyes closed with each bob a nod of reverence to the drums. We are a people of ritual which is to say our gods are born with expectation. Necks tilt as they take in this god's gift, an ichor of truth-telling. But a god is never without his tricks. Pink flesh crackling, he crosses finger over left. Everything is a joke to he who sheaths his fists. But even air and intent is enough to scar. There are ways to command outside of words. So stomachs curl in response and mouths open the seven plagues. There is something lost in truth. I, reanimated, mourn who I am and excavate what was with two fingers into cavern. I need not for liquid catalyst. I spew with determination. Sparkling and new, he chooses me. He chooses me and begins to cut. He carves until I am lightened. Arms, thighs, and stomach. Layered slabs for the hungry dogs. An indent for longevity. Each mark a reminder that a gift does not come free. Another cut for beauty. And so he goes. In everyone lies a god of death. And he carves -- we carve -- until I am perfect.

I CRY TO THE STEPS OF A POETRY PROMPT

SPEAK THE NUMBERS AS PART OF THE LINE

1. I bow to the god of realizations.
2. I was made new, believer.
3. They stir every time I speak their names.
4. Every card I pull is a Bisayan deity.
5. I return to these gods of my people.
6. I kiss my tarot deck thank you.
7. I visit a Tagalog seer and she asks where my family is from.
8. She hears my spirit team and can't understand them.
9. I cry at this meaning,
10. Auntie Linda, Auntie Marionetta, Lola Cadia, Lolo Jose.
11. Bisayan as smirk and quick wit.
12. Cebuano as puffed chest and quicker mouth.
13. Bisayan blood is warm and thrumming.
14. Bisayan blood is loud, is holding.
15. Bisdak as chant, as prayer.
16. Remember, I bow to the god of realizations.
17. My Tagalog ancestors continue their tradition of abandonment.
18. I cold at this new meaning.
19. My Tagalog ancestors echo my mother.
20. My tongue all Tagalog.
21. My tongue wishing itself back to Cebu.
22. Toward this warmth, butterflied opening in my chest,
23. Because the seer smiling, says Lolo is here.
24. Seer smiling, says Lolo visits me often.
25. Seer smiling, says Lolo forgives me.

                              Did you feel that?

26. The crack of an earthquake is good luck where I'm from.
27. I end the session, island melting into wave,
28. A rock releasing the way a fist becomes an open palm.

LIAM NEESON NARRATES THE BIG BANG, & I KNOW I'LL BE OKAY

It's a relief to be so small. The world is so big and beautiful, I brush myself beneath its layers. We are 13 million years separated from joyous birth. I see my path diverge from its tree and accept its gnarling. Or is it rooting? It is brown and tender. Knotted and blooming. I am given everything I need, which includes truth. I agree to accept the unraveling and sob with the goats and oxes. It's okay. Mermaid horned deity of wisdom says it's so. What's one unanswered text? What's one obligatory call?

I've waited enough.
Sometimes love is a standstill.
Sometimes love is good as is.

It sits in its box comfortably.

I'm ready to go.

The path winds back down to the entrance,

and the doors only a few feet away.

WHEN I OPENED MY EYES AND I WAS BACK IN MILPITAS, 2016

I brushed against the hand of god at the turn of summer.
I walked with her towards Ocean Supermarket,
the streets leaning inward at her arrival.
In the here and then,
we light candles for her and her siblings,
a pantheon dipped in wax.
Here, we refigure the body to our landscape.
This body which is ours a divine right.
Here, we find the beauty in bodily alchemy.
Every line and stroke on our fingers proof
we are the beginning and forever.
Here, amongst another, we are safe.
Here, we all bear the hands of god.
raise our arms, creating with united
hums the sun.
a kaleidoscope of hands.
One day 20%
will be zero.

I look at the trees, and they bow at the
procession.
We honor the
pilgrimage.
thank the sun for each of its
rays, which adorn her
forehead like a crown.
They will always remember.
gather these rays and think of Septembers

ELEGY TO [NEURODIVERGENT] SELF

I.
um. the crows perch the brick.
um. somedays, i prefer a crevice to, um.
a space too, too wide and um. two years
ago um. my sister injected um. fillers into her
top lip um a suction cup gloss that um.
proclaimed she was um. more beautiful um.
and therefore um. value differs from person
to person so i crumble at um. the face of love
um. and warm hands um. i'm [always] talking
about hands um. and the marvel of its ability
um. to outreach and um. overcome and hold and

II.
um, want. um, isn't that [always] um, the problem?
um, i think i was um, going somewhere with hands
because um, i wish i knew where i um, was going
to the store or back home um, or i stand in place
um, thinking and thinking and thinking and thinking
and not moving or moving only thinking um, why
do you think that this is something um, i was going
somewhere and then i forgot um, i try to flint fire
from fern and spring um, when i was young i um,
refused naps because i wanted to learn about the
mysterious vowel y and um, i was [always] one
um, to seek the rules to break them um, even
when um, i wasn't out looking to break them um,

III.

um things that are misshapen are um [always]
made out to be broken um i went to the farmer's
market with lola um i think i get this from
her um we circle the stalls swearing to all the
gods um that we'll remember at the next rotation
the same way the sun forgets every four years um
how to do um its job but um that's something i
um tell myself because um i'm always talking
um to myself um [always] trying to catch up um
[always] trying to slow down [always] [always] um
did you know that repetition is a form of violence?
um did you know that i want to fill the silence?
um, a window never opens on its own, and um
I've decided it's better to die crowed in sunlight um
in drafty afternoon um here atop unfeeling brick.

RECOVERING CATHOLIC POETRY

Where I call me Jesus,

Jesus 8 years bone-etched.

Jesus and eyes can't outlive the past.

Jesus, the boys will only rave over that which they crave.

Jesus twin, as stomach and ribs,

Jesus' ribs which skin erupts.

Jesus' ribs now cloaked, each rib a crown.

Jesus' skin I know is separate,

Jesus' skin more than my own,

Jesus I curse the expansion of me.

Jesus and the Presumptuous Girl, renaming herself Jesus to match.

Jesus, as Girl, spares the Presumptuous Boy, stuck on a stick poor ideal.

Jesus, absolve this distance.

Jesus forgive the laughter.

"BEFORE I WAS A POET, I WAS A LINEAGE."
—KB BROOKINS

One day, this kid will be a kid.
One day, this kid will shed all earth sign.
Which is to say, one day I will shed snake coil.
One day, this kid won't be a third.
One day, this kid will have chaperones and PTA meetings.
One day, this kid will be middle, will be last.
One day, this kid will know how to sing songs with abandon.
One day, mountains will descend.
One day, this day will come.
One day, we'll be dash liberated glass slipper.
One day, this kid will find kindness.

One day, this kid will choose to settle in it.
One day, this kid will live shoulders recobbled.
One day, this kid will learn want.
One day, this kid will be _____.

WHAT IF WE DIDN'T DIE?

We would move faster than atoms and grow beyond trees. Our houses would shelter acres and acres of branches. Our skin would still bruise but bear three arms, the more to bring pagkain to all of our lolas. We are eternal. We are a force. All of my lolas exhale and with it they call upon the seasons change. All of my splinters never ruptured nor cut anyone.

I am smooth.

                                                              I am whole.

I would never need Google Translate because all of my translators carry four tongues. I would never need Google Translate kasi nandito sila sa dila ko. Nandito wala si Ingles. Kay ania sila sa akong dila. Wala dinhi ang English. I would always speak in twos. My Lolo would talk forever. Into the night, across the day. His eyes would become purple. As Amethyst. As royalty. He would know his father. And he would know me. I wouldn't need memory. The wrinkles in my brain could unfold and recrease. And it would be okay. I would be more than okay. And I would know them all.

Scorpio Rising

Ocean has eyes   In another imagining of the world, waves have wings.

Ocean has eyes   I only know because the ocean is ancestor,

Ocean has eyes   An accumulation of tribes riding its waves and currents.

All of its salt and all its power. It decides to separate or bind. Sea carries all their secrets in her abysmal womb. I confess to the sea my shadows and watch them sink into her depth. In these moments I see pupils of my lineage in her waves. Mother and mother before her. Their angles echo back in my cheekbones. They catch a glimmer of light as I catch the sight of them. My feet kissed sacred, my hands gently splash salt water into the air in celebration and prayer. May we always remember. May we always ritual.

I AM ASKED, WHAT DOES JOY LOOK LIKE BEYOND SURVIVAL?

Lolo is here. He is always here in stillness. The sharp contrast of his voice to the trees. In the driveway of our family home, he waved at every passerby. I cherish the dollar he gave me for chichirria and mourn that I spent it. I don't know if our bodies ever knew rest. Beyond our psoas muscles and shoulders. I know the body keeps the score. Imagination is the only refuge we have. How many more years do we give to survival?

I walk from the elementary school where I work to my car and gasp at the miracle that is leaves against wind. So this is the divine timing they speak of. I walk through, a personal curtain. For a second, I'm the queen Lolo promised I was when I was 4 years old, plastic bucket on my head, the frayed hand-me-down duster swishing against my legs. Mouth open to the wind is the closest I've been to touching God. This is my kingdom. This is our kingdom. What if we stayed so still we sank into the earth? What if there were more than 10,000 leagues? I count my blessings by the number of iced coffees and books I have in my room. I watch my sister breathe and know that each intake is a gift. My lolo is no longer here, but joy remains where the pot is hot. I look over my shoulder and my lola's back is straight. I open my hands and find daisies in my palms. I arrange them in a vase for my mother. I drape myself under layers of blankets. How much more can I say to define joy as safety? Where this is joy, there is surrender. And in this surrender, I let it carry me to sleep.

I was Born on a Sunday

Matcha makes morning.
The birds visit the rosemary,
& I tell them Lola will return
in two days. I separate the years
by its shape & I am surprised
at my strength. For I swum to its
lowest hues, still found my way to
surface. The god to whom I pray
was once a girl who broke stride
during a race to help another. A
girl who knew grit. The god to
whom I pray was once alone,
hands on blue leather nodding
to a white coat and transducer.
This god, no longer girl, is still
here. Not only here, but knowing
joy. I watch the trees sway to
my laugh at four, sixteen, &
twenty-seven. All these years it
took to remind me I'm not alone.
I hold his hand, & then mine.
Tomorrow, I'll wake & make
matcha. Tomorrow, I'll know
I've a life well-lived.

Publisher's Note

The Tagalog and Cebuano phrases found throughout the collection are translated into English in the following Translation Index.

We translate these phrases into English for inclusivity purposes in respect to our non-Tagalog, non-Cebuano speaking readers, particularly BIPOC and non-Tagalog, non-Cebuano Filipinxao readers. We also translate these phrases in order to adhere to the requirements set by some book distributors.

We are aware of the compromise we make in order to make this art more accessible to a wider audience. In translating these phrases, we participate in a global market that continues to be dictated by Western- and English-supremacist practices. We are also aware that these simple, direct translations of words fall short in communicating their cultural weight and meaning.

We acknowledge the history of translating devices used violently as tools of white gaze revisionism, for the cultural erasure and othering of non-Western, Global South, and diaspora art. This includes the related practice in the United States publishing industry of italicizing words from non-English languages. Our current policy is not to italicize these words.

As cultural discourse, translation methods, and language resources evolve with the times, so may our formatting and translating practices at Sampaguita Press. It is our dream and goal to be able to have our titles commercially available and translated into different languages other than English, for greater language and literary equity.

TRANSLATION INDEX

The page numbers follow the print edition of *The Language of Unbreaking*. Words may appear multiple times throughout the book. Here we list their first appearance.

Because the author is Cebuano and Tagalog we have denoted the language as Cebuano, Tagalog, or "both" as there are distinct differences between the two languages. However, we understand words share meaning across the 177+ Philippine languages, and acknowledge this kapamilya of Philippine languages even though we cannot name them all.

Cebuano is a dialect of the Bisaya language which is spoken in the Visayas or the Visayan region of the Philippines. Bisaya is also known as Binisaya. Bisayan languages include Cebuano, Hiligaynon, Waray, and Davaoeño.

Additionally, in some poems, the grammar is not correct. This is intentional. This is the result of assimilation and the process of reclamation of a Filipinx in diaspora relearning their family languages.

Lola (14): grandmother; both

Paksiw na isda (14): fish cooked in vinegar; both

Lolo (15): grandfather; both

Tapon (16): throw away; both

Asa imong kapwa? (16): where is your kapwa; Cebuano

Kapwa (16): fellowship, togetherness, kindred, core value in Filipino culture that describes sharing an identity and caring for others; both

Asawa (17): spouse; Tagalog; wife; Cebuano

Parejong ngipin sila sa mga tiger (17): they have the same teeth as tigers; Tagalog

Kasi (17): because; both

Sila (17): them; both

Mga puti (17): white people

Itong (17): this; Tagalog

Di ba (17): right?; Tagalog

Apo (17):grandchildren; both

Ano ba (17): what?; Tagalog

Sino ba? (17): who?; both

Ng ingles kami (17): our English; Tagalog

Salamat sa diyos (17): Thank god; Tagalog

Ninang (19): godmother; both

Tong tong tong pakitong-kitong (20): originally a Cebuano folk song depicting the movement of a giant crab that is delicious to eat but difficult to catch because it pinches

Mare (21): shortened version of kumare, female friend; both

Lola at Lolo (22): grandmother and grandfather; Tagalog

Magkakarne (22): butchers; both

Nay (22): shorthand of nanay meaning mother; Tagalog

Singit (22): groin; Tagalog

Ito Na, Para Kay Lola, Amping (24): this, for grandma, always; Cebuano

Gumagising si Lola mga 9 o 10 sa umaga (24): grandma wakes up around 9 or 10 in the morning; Tagalog

Akyat ni Lola sa kwarto ko kasi umaga sa akin (24): grandma came up to my room, because morning for me; Tagalog

Kusog kaayo (24): very strong; Cebuano

Dodong (24): term of endearment for a young man or boy in the Visayas; Cebuano

Inday (24): term of endearment for a young woman or girl in the Visayas; Cebauno

Manang (24): term of respect to address an older female relative, older sister, similar to Tagalog's "Ate"; Cebuano

Talsik (24): splash, splatter; Tagalog

Gahi (24): hard, rough; Cebauno

Kundiman (24): traditional Filipino love song used to subvertly express patriotism during Spanish colonial period, evolved from folk tradition to a formal art song, in 3/4 time verse that starts on a minor chord and progresses to major chords.

Uulan (25): will rain; Tagalog

Pare (25): shortened version of kumpare; male friend; both

Bahay de pan (25): house of bread; Tagalog

Pan de buhay (25): bread of life; Tagalog

Hija de pan (25): daughter of bread; both

Ambot (25): I don't know, or I know nothing; Cebuano

Bitaw (25): anyway, indeed; Cebuano

Tsismis (25): gossip; both

Ate (25): term of respect to address an older female relative, older sister, similar to Cebuano's "Manang"; Tagalog

Kuya (25): term of respect to address an older male relative, older brother, similar to Cebuano's "Manong"; Tagalog

Manong (25): term of respect to address an older male relative, older brother, similar to Tagalog's "Kuya"; Cebuano

Manong ug mga kaibigan (25): older male relative and friends; Cebuano

Ug (25): and; Cebuano

Kasi meaning yung yan (26): because that's what it means; Tagalog

Paksiw na Isda ni Lola (27): grandma's fish paksiw; both

Tinik (27): bones of fish, also means thorn; Tagalog

Pupunta dito, galing sa Tondo (36): coming here from Tondo; Tagalog

Simbang gabi (36): night mass, Catholic tradition that involves a series of nine masses leading up to Christmas; both

Dami (39): a lot; Tagalog

Pawis (39): sweat; Tagalog

Aso (39): dog; Tagalog

Tongits (40): card game similar to rummy, tonk, and mahjong; both

Sakit (50): sickness; both

Kasamas (53): multiple meanings depending on language and part of speech, noun: companion, verb: "to be together", preposition: with; both

Utang na loob (55): Filipino concept of eternal debt to others who do a favor for you, sense of obligation to return a favor; both

Simbang Gabi para sa mga Puti (60): night mass for white people; Tagalog

Ano daw? (60): what did they say?; Tagalog

Bakit meron silang Simbang Gabi sa Easter? (60): why do they have night mass for Easter; Tagalog

Ano ba yan? (60): what is that?; Tagalog

Pasensya (60): pardon me, I'm sorry; Tagalog

Ingat (60): be careful, always take care; Tagalog

Ang Tatay ng Nanay ko, hinawak niya ang kamay ko. Ang sabi niya (60): my mom's dad, he held my hand, he said; Tagalog

Sinabi ko (60): I said; Tagalog

Kuyate (67): portmanteau of Kuya and Ate, a modern attempt to be more inclusive of gender-expansive folks; Tagalog

Kulit (67): persistence, stubbornness, pesky; Tagalog

Wala ko kabalo (71): I don't know; Cebuano

Mana kay tatay ko kasi (76): I'm like my dad because; Tagalog

Alum ko na (76): I know now; Tagalog

Gikan kanimo, kami natawo. Usa ko ka bata sa kadagatan sa Turtle Island (84): from you, we are born. I am a child from the sea of Turtle Island; Cebuano

Bata ko sa kadagatan nga nangandoy sa Sugbo (84): I am a child of the sea who longs for Cebu; Cebuano

Bisdak (86): Bisaya Dako, dako meaning big, big Bisaya, slang term referring people born and raised in the Visayas; Cebuano

Pagkain (93): food; Tagalog

kasi nandito sila sa dila ko (93): because they're here on my tongue; Tagalog

Nandito wala si Ingles (93): here there's no English; Tagalog

Kay ania sila sa akong dila (93): they're here on my tongue; Cebuano

Wala dinhi ang English (93): here there's no English; Cebuano

Author's Notes

Concept: Reflection of self as separate/part of a family; sections are divided by meaning and interaction of familial last names.

Last Names Explored & Meaning(s):
Labra - Unbreakable (family lore); structure corresponding to a lip, esp. of a crustacean or insect; cutting, carving wood or stone
Aguila - Eagle
Masucol - to fight (family lore); inspiring, master of their own destiny, intuitive
Aranas - Spider/spiderweb, scratch/scrape/claw/claw at, chandelier
Bautista - baptist
Romano - person belonging to Rome, cheese
Galang - respect, reference, polite behavior, courtesy, deference to those in authority
Lopez - wolf
Nolasco - from St. Peter of Nolasco
Cortes - courteous, polite, refined person

If you want to know who I am, is written after Carlos Bulosan and Lorenz Mazon Dumuk

I'm mourning on a Tuesday is written after Billy Rey Belcourt

Ito Na Para Kay Lola, Amping is written after Lorenz Mazon Dumuk, Jason Magabo Perez, and Maria Bolaños. This ekphrastic poem was first born in conversation with the painting, Yosi Con Abuela by Rafa Esparza. In 2023, its installment was homed in the San José Museum of Art

Enough is written after Noreen Ocampo's "self-portrait as reasons i write"

"In my grief, I've changed & that's okay" is written after after Maria Bolaños, Barton Fink, and the djinn from Three Thousand Years of Longing

The Body is Our Body Until It is Not Our Body is written after Victoria Chang and in response to painter, Riva Lehrer's, "Coloring Book"

Terabithia is written after Ellie Labampa

How will you / have you prepare(d) for his death? is written after Chen Chen and Lorenz Mazon Dumuk

Lola says wala ko kabalo but what she really means is she doesn't remember is written after Lorenz Mazon Dumuk and Maria Bolaños

Deepest Condolences to the Labra Family is written after Gemma Aurora Garcia, Akwaeke Emezi, and Maria Bolaños

Only an (Aguila) Labra Would Fight God, Which is to Say Only I Would Fight God was originally published in the Midnight Mass Anthology

I keep saying the same thing but it's okay's form is after Helli Fang's "Landscape is Falling" in the chapbook, Village of Knives

When I Opened My Eyes and I was Back in Milpitas, 2016 is written in memory of Nguyen Thi Mai Natalie and in Response to Cassils' "The Resilience of the 20%". 2 versions of **When I Opened My Eyes and I was Back in Milpitas, 2016** were published in a chapbook published by The Montalvo Center for the Arts and by East Side Magazine. In the Montalvo Center of the Arts chapbook, the poem is titled For Trans Day of Remembrance. This poem is after Hala Alyan

What If We Didn't Die? is written after Bayani Bala and Maria Bolaños

Scorpio Rising is co-authored with Lorenz Mazon Dumuk. The form follows Helli Fang's "Genesis" in the chapbook, Village of Knives.

I am asked, what does joy look like beyond survival? is written after Lorenz Mazon Dumuk

I was Born on a Sunday was written after Christian Aldana

Acknowledgements

To Lolo, eternally.

To the band, The Story So Far. Thank you for your music which teaches me how to write my own by way of poetry.

To my inaanak, Chloe. You are spitfire and wit! Ninang Nini loves you!

To all the pets I have ever known and loved. You live nestled in my heart. I think of you with every squeaky toy, tree, and gust of wind I experience.

To the beta readers: Lillian Rankin, Yvonne Vallejo, Nicole Cadelina, Jenelle DeCosta, Gretchen Henderson, & Dallas Atlas. Thank you for being the first to witness this child in its early stages. Thank you for your care and attention.

To the blurb writers: Tshaka Campbell, antmen pimentel mendoza, Aileen Cassinetto, Arlene Biala, Lorenz Mazon Dumuk, & Belana Labra. Thank you for the time, effort, and kindness you put into your blurbs.

To this book's amazing cover and internal artist, Chris Sicat. Thank you for sharing your art and allowing it to be in conversation with these poems.

To Judy Dennis & Kelly Sicat. My dear mentors, role models, and friends. I'm in awe of your brightness, smarts, and warmth. May I one day embody even an iota of your presence.

To Montalvo Arts Center. Many of these poems were born in studio I call my "own", my "beloved." This space is a magical one, and I'm graetful to be a part of this community.

To SVCreates, Local Color, & Poetry Center San Jose. Thank you for providing opportunities to help this work flourish. Thank you for the gift you give to the creatives here in San José and the South Bay.

To my parents. Thank you for the gift of life. I continue to learn from the both of you. May you both find peace and joy in your "young" adulthood.

To my siblings: Jamie and Jaden. Jam & Jad, everything will be okay, I promise. And if not, Ate K is only a phone call away (just not too many phone calls, please, I'm old now.)

To my dear cousin and friend, Belana. Lana, you are a joy to chat and spend time with. Though we are apart, when we reunite, it's as though no time has passed at all. I'm ecstatic to share art with you.

To Lola. Thank you for being my event buddy. You make all these shows, open mics, and features more enjoyable with your presence. Gihigugma ko ikaw.

To Auntie Sugar. You have been and will always be my second mother. I think of you on every plane, train, and bus ride. You fuel my adventurous side. Thank you for teaching me bravery.

To the WildPKids: PinPin, Baby, Perse, & Artemi. My darling babies. I know you're not babies anymore, but let Ate K baby you a little longer. Thank you for being my cousins and my kids. I love you immensely.

To Rick Barot. I applied to PLU because of you. I can't tell you how inspiring it was to see you, a queer Filipino poet, directing the Rainier's Writing Workshop low-residency MFA. Your presence reassured me that my writing would be understood and guided in a way that it would not only grow, but be cared for. Maraming salamat.

Thanks to my RWW mentors thus far: torrin a. greathouse and Oliver de la Paz. Thank you for being in my school of poetics/poetic family tree.

To antmen pimentel mendoza. Ate, thank you for guiding the way in the RWW program. I can't tell you how much I look up to you. I truly am following you as your shadow, and I'm honored to do so.

To Dallas Atlas, Kalehua Kim, Eric "Papa Loch" Lochridge, Erin Allen & Ate antmen. Your collective talent continues to amaze and inspire me. Thank you for adopting me into your cohort.

To my dear cohort: Sharina Black, Gloria Bromberg, Eric Callahan, Krista Lee Hanson, Kerry J Heckman, Dabu Johansson, Myrna CG Mibus, Marnie Ritchie, Marty Salgado, Travis Timmons, Cheryl Waitkevich, & Miłosz Konstanty Szyszka. Each of you are so unique and stunning in the work that you do and joy that you share. I'm so lucky to be in this MFA with you all. Go cohort 20!

To TDS mga kasama ko: Maria Bolaños, Butch Schwartzkopf, Christian Aldana, Czaerra Galicinao Ucol, David Maduli, Hari Alluri, Jason Magabo Perez, & Rachelle Cruz. Thank you for continuously holding space and throwing down. I'm speechless at each of you, you all a force to behold.

To the Sampaguita Press & Marías at Sampaguitas staff: thank you all for sharing this dream, for this shared camaraderie across the digital space. Here's to publishing more books in 2, 5, 10 years and on, puhon!

To Ate Che, Chris, Maria, & David, my LA pamilya. I miss you all so dearly whenever we are apart. Our time together truly feels like family time. I laugh to myself at the "Whitney" incident all the time. Until we beat the next escape room again!

To Reginald Imbat. Reggie. Julianato. Wedge. My best friend! You're getting old now, man. It's been 15 years since we met and became friends. I look forward to spending more movie nights, food outings, vacations, and fun times together. Thank you for the blessing that is our friendship.

To Miłosz Konstanty Szyszka. Milo, my dear friend! You're so incredibly talented, intillegent, and kind. I look forward to residency every year because it means I get to spend more time with you! Thank you for our text exchanges and FaceTime calls.

To Ellie Lopez & Lorenz Mazon Dumuk. My water sign kaibigans / amigos. My Bay Area poets! Mailobs! There is no better place to share

Mariah Carey or Bad Bunny memes. Both of your writing steers mine. May we always be in the same poetic family tree.

To Manang Arlene Biala, Manang Janice Lobo Sapigao, Mighty Mike McGee, Tshaka Campbell, Scorpiana Xlent, and Lorenz Mazon Dumuk. My beloved San Jose poets. My 408 poets. Thank you for your tutelage, love, and care. Thank you for letting me be a part. Y'all always take me to the parking lot.

To mare Kelly Ritter. My pop punk sibling. Your ferocity is unmatched! I'm lucky to be a recipient of your care and love. You inspire me to be better everyday, not only with SamPress, but with our health and fitness. Thank you for holding me in all vulnerabilities. I hope I can continue to do the same for you. I'm so glad to have met you and know you.

To mare Maria Bolaños. Mars. I can't begin to touch the depth of my love for you. I've always been the more weepy, sappy one, and for you, I will hold back! Please know that I thank the Universe for the steadiness of your soul and the howling we share in all of our conversations: Zoom, chat, and in-person alike. There is no Keana without Maria, in literary spheres or otherwise. Thank you for being my pinsan, kaibigan, and mare.

Eric, my love. In this life and the next, in this universe and the next, we are leaf.

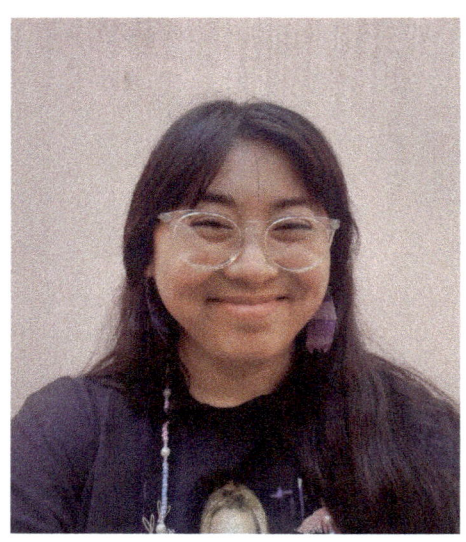

ABOUT THE AUTHOR

Keana Aguila Labra (they/them/she/her) is a queer Cebuana Tagalog Filipinx genre- and genderfluid/non-binary poet, editor, playwright, and writer in diaspora residing on stolen Ohlone Tamyen land. She works to provide a safe literary space for underserved and underrepresented communities as co-Editor-in-Chief of literary magazine, *Marías at Sampaguitas* and co-Founder of the BIPOC/LGBTQIA+ focused independent publishing house, Sampaguita Press. She served as one of the Honorary Santa Clara County Poets Laureate in October 2021 alongside Lorenz Mazon Dumuk. They were the SVCreates SVLaureate & Content Emerging Artist for 2023 and is a proud recipient of the Lucas Artists Residency Program Fellowship through Montalvo Arts Center. She is the author of the poetry chapbooks, *Natalie* (Nightingale & Sparrow, 2020), *No Saints* (Lazy Adventurer Publishing, 2020), *Mohilak* (Fahmidan Co. & Publishing, 2021) and *Kanunay* (Violet & The Bird, 2022). *The Language of Unbreaking* (Sampaguita Press, 2025) is their first full-length publication.

About the Artist

Chris Sícat is a Bay Area artist, curator and educator. Sícat's paintings and sculptures highlight natural objects as a platform for performance based art making. Sícat obsessively and meticulously covers pieces of minimally sculpted redwood with graphite using hundreds of pencils per each piece. His watercolor paintings venture to both abstraction and representational. The works become visual reflections of the internal and exterior engagement of the physical body.

Sícat has exhibited his works internationally at Paper Gallery in Manchester, U.K.; Gallery Lara in Tokyo, Japan; Intramuros Museum in Manila, Philippines. His work has also shown at K. Imperial Fine Arts, de Saisset Museum at Santa Clara University, Big Basin State Park, Palo Alto Art Center, Southern Exposure, and Intersection for the Arts in the Bay Area.

Cover art and all interior artworks in watercolor.

LAND ACKNOWLEDGEMENT

This book was written on the lands of the Ohlone Tamyen People. It was produced on the lands of the Ohlone People.

As settlers on Turtle Island, the staff at Sampaguita Press acknowledge we are on the stolen sacred lands of these Peoples. We remember their connection to these regions and give thanks for the opportunity to live, teach, and learn in their traditional homelands. May we create connections with them, and may we learn Indigenous protocols to become honorable stewards of the land.

We encourage you, Reader, to:

• Amplify the voices of Indigenous people leading grassroots change movements
• Donate your time and money to Indigenous-led organizations
• Politically support the Land Back Movement

In line with these encouragements, Sampaguita Press supports Indigenous art and donates a portion of Press funds raised to Indigenous-led organizations.

In reflecting on our own lives and remembering our family histories, we must remember the legacies of colonialism that we have benefitted from and continue to benefit from as settler-colonialists.

From Palestine to the Philippines, none of us are free until all of us are free.

About Sampaguita Press

Sampaguita Press is an independent micropress publishing house based in San Jose, California. We publish works by and for Black, Indigenous, and POC artists. We acknowledge the intersections of identity and support the LGBTQIA+ folk/x in the Black, Indigenous, and POC communities as well.

Sampaguita Press was founded in 2021 by poets and creatives who wanted to create a space and platform for ourselves, our peers, and other fellow voices who are underrepresented in mainstream publishing.

We strive to inspire progressive change. We acknowledge that change is made with solidarity. We honor and nurture the relationships between our fellow communities. We especially seek works that broaden perspectives and foster understanding.

We believe in racial and social equity. We acknowledge that Western literature and publishing are still overwhelmingly white spaces, and we are committed to amplifying underrepresented voices by providing attention and care to artists who may not have access to traditional publishing spaces.

We are an intersectionally feminist & womanist, inclusive press. We prioritize Black, Indigenous, and POC artists of all genders. We discourage hegemonic narratives; hierarchical structures; and supremacist, assimilationist, and normative messaging.

We are a safe literary & linguistic space, and we welcome chapbook submissions in non-English languages.

We support Indigenous rights and sovereignty over the land known as the United States. Our support goes out to the Indigenous groups everywhere in the world who have been harmed, silenced, and displaced. We encourage our readers to learn about and support Indigenous Peoples.

www.ingramcontent.com/pod-product-compliance
Lightning Source LLC
Chambersburg PA
CBHW051323120626
46547CB00015B/2363